TUTANKHAMUN

Egypt's Boy Pharaoh

Written by Elena Marcos Alvarez
Translated by Rebecca Neal

History 50MINUTES.com

TUTANKHAMUN

KEY INFORMATION

- **Born:** between 1346 and 1332 BCE in Akhetaton, Egypt.
- **Died:** between 1325 and 1313 BCE in Thebes, Egypt.
- **Main achievements:** the restoration of polytheism in Egypt after the monotheistic regime of his father.

INTRODUCTION

Tutankhamun is one of the best-known pharaohs of ancient Egypt, and for good reason: when his tomb was discovered by the British archaeologist Howard Carter (1874-1939) on 4 November 1922, it was still intact and perfectly preserved after almost 3000 years. The priceless treasure within inspired both awe and fear due to the legend that Tutankhamun's tomb is cursed. Indeed, several members of the team studying the tomb died suddenly and in unexplained circumstances after it was discovered.

Because of the treasure that filled his tomb, the Tutankhamun of the popular imagination is a majestic pharaoh, but the realities of this young sovereign's life remain virtually unknown. In this guide, we will explore the struggles that marked his life, the way he lived, the cause of his death and the true story behind the mythical curse in order to gain a real insight into the life of this mysterious pharaoh.

BIOGRAPHY

Gilded wooden bust of Tutankhamun discovered by Howard Carter in 1922.

ROYAL BIRTH AND CHILDHOOD

Prince Tutankhamun was born in the royal palace in Tell el-Amarna, Upper Egypt, between 1346 and 1332 BCE. He was the son of the pharaoh Akhenaton (date of birth unknown, date of death c. 1338/37 BCE) and an anonymous woman whose mummy is known as the Younger Lady to differentiate her from the bodies of a very young boy and an older woman which were found in her tomb. The Younger Lady is probably an unknown sister of Akhenaton, or his cousin and principal wife Nefertiti (c. 1370-c. 1333 BCE).

CONSANGUINEOUS MARRIAGE IN ANCIENT EGYPT

Carrying out genetic identification on mummies from this period is often difficult because of the prevalence of consanguineous marriage (marriage between blood relatives) during the 18th Dynasty in order to avoid diluting the royal bloodline.

Tutankhamun was born between the 12th and the 14th year of his father's reign and had an uneventful childhood, either in the royal palace in Tell el-Amarna with his parents or in the cities of Thebes and Memphis, where he was raised by his wet nurse or by tutors. However, few documents about Tutankhamun's life prior to his accession to the throne have survived, so we do not have many exact details about the young prince's childhood.

ACCESSION TO THE THRONE

Tutankhamun came to the throne around 1340 BCE, after the short reign of his elder sister Meritaten (c. 1350-c. 1336/35 BCE), although some believe that the queen at this time was Nefertiti. In any case, she only ruled over Egypt for a few years. When she died (it is unclear whether she died of natural causes or was murdered), Tutankhamun acceded to the throne, although he was only six or eight years old, to become the 11th pharaoh of the 18th Dynasty of Egypt (mid-16th century BCE-late 13th century BCE). His reign marked the high-water mark of this ancient civilisation and the beginning of the New Kingdom of Egypt (1500-1000 BCE).

When Tutankhamun was born, he was known as Tutankhaten, which means "the living image of Aten" in homage to the only god his father worshiped. When the young prince came to the throne, the god Amun and his priests were restored to their preeminent place after the reign of Akhenaton and his monotheistic worship of Aten. He also changed his name to Tutankhamun, meaning "the living image of Amun". In doing so, he mirrored his father, who had been known as Amenhotep IV before changing his name to Akhenaton.

MARRIAGE

After becoming pharaoh, Tutankhamun married his elder sister Ankhesanamun (born as Ankhesenpaaten, c. 1349-c. 1323 BCE), the royal couple's third daughter. According to estimates, the young pharaoh was around seven years old when he married his sister, who was aged around 12 at the time. Child marriages were relatively common in ancient Egypt, and although marriages between brothers and sisters with the same mother were much rarer, they were tolerated in royal families under the New Kingdom of Egypt.

This practice prevented wars of succession between the heirs to the throne, who were often the offspring of different royal marriages. However, many of Tutankhamun and Ankhesanamun's brothers and sisters had already died at a young age, which meant that Ankhesanamun may have been the only other person with a claim to the throne. She was Tutankhamun's only known wife, but he almost certainly had a harem and several secondary wives, as polygamy was an established tradition in ancient Egypt.

THE PHARAOH'S HEIRS

Tutankhamun only had two children, and they were both stillborn. Archaeologists know about them because they were buried with their father in the tomb discovered by Howard Carter. Both children were daughters, and died during the fourth and seventh months of pregnancy. Since Tutankhamun died at the age of just 20 in circumstances which remain unclear, leaving no heirs, his former tutor Ay (12th pharaoh of the 18th Dynasty) assumed leadership of Egypt.

| Howard Carter in Chicago, January 1924.

RELIGIOUS AND POLITICAL CONTEXT

THE RELIGIOUS CONTEXT BEFORE TUTANKHAMUN'S REIGN

Before Tutankhamun became pharaoh of Egypt, his father Akhenaton sent shockwaves through the country by adopting a new monotheistic religion dedicated to the sun god Aten, which was completely at odds Egypt's traditional polytheistic practices.

This religious reform began in around 1343 BCE following internal disagreements in the upper echelons of power. The pharaoh then decided to promote a religion which would be represented by him alone in order to keep a firm grip on the state, his people and religious customs. This new religion was dedicated to the sun-disc Aten, meaning the tangible manifestation of the sun. It was therefore a monotheistic belief system based on a radical form of the solar religion that was already widespread at this time.

Anyone who has already been to Egypt will attest to the fact that the sun, with is oppressive heat, can play a major role in the inhabitants' daily lives. This new religion was therefore based on the exclusive worship not of a human-like deity, but of the sun, the star that illuminates and heats the earth. As a result, the sun-disc became the only god in Egypt.

This radical religious reform was pushed through relatively quickly: in less than two years, Akhenaton ordered the destruction of the names of the main gods, including Amun, on the temples. He disbanded all religious bodies that were not dedicated to the worship of Aten, left all the temples to fall into disrepair and built a new capital named Akhetaton in homage to his chosen god.

EGYPT'S REAL LEADERS

Tutankhamun was still only a child when he became leader of Upper and Lower Egypt. This meant that the real power lay in the hands of two other men: his tutor Ay (date of birth unknown, date of death c. 1320 BCE) and the general Horemheb (date of birth unknown, date of death c. 1300 BCE).

Horemheb was only slightly less powerful than the king, and it appears that he was the real leader of Egypt, especially in matters of foreign policy. His tomb in Saqqara lists his many responsibilities: general, head of the troops, messenger to the king, leader of the entire country, and more. In written sources, he is described as though he were a sovereign, with terms and expressions that are usually reserved for the ruling pharaoh.

SIGNIFICANT REFORM

The first major decision made during Tutankhamun's reign was to restore the old religion, which was polytheistic with Amun as the principal deity. The body of priests dedicated to Amun, which had been dissolved some ten years previously, was re-established. At the same time, the religion introduced by the former pharaoh was outlawed and all traces of Atenism were erased from the country. During Tutankhamun's reign, the temples' coffers swelled slowly but surely. Their wealth was mainly based on the size of their cattle herds, which spread across Egypt and into Nubia.

This renewed religious activity was also very beneficial to Egypt's artisans, who were mainly based in Memphis and whose main clients were the king and the temples. From now on, they could produce objects for the worship of all Egypt's divinities.

The Precinct of Amun-Re in Karnak was a very important temple enclosure, and also played a major economic role in the New Kingdom of Egypt, to such an extent that it was probably the richest institution in the country. The reopening of the temple was a powerful symbolic gesture by Tutankhamun, and the financial benefits it brought must have been warmly welcomed by Egypt's citizens.

TURBULENT FOREIGN RELATIONS

Unlike his predecessors, Tutankhamun did not distinguish himself through his foreign policy. Relations with the rest of the Near East were more or less stable, but the rival kingdoms fought among one another, without any one country gaining the upper hand. The Hittite empire, which stretched across Anatolia in western Asia, was growing in power, as was Assyria in northern Mesopotamia, which would soon become the dominant power in the Near East. Mitanni (a kingdom in the Near East, to the north-east of present-day Syria) and Babylon (an ancient city in Mesopotamia, located in present-day Iraq) still existed, but were far less powerful than they had once been.

Most of Egypt's problems in foreign affairs came from the Hittites. During Akhenaton's reign, the relationship between the two countries was already fraught, and wars frequently broke out between them. However, this did not seem to bother Akhenaton, and he made no effort to maintain peace in his kingdom. Under the rule of Tutankhamun's elder sister Meritaten, diplomatic relations between the two countries improved significantly, particularly because of an arranged marriage between the Egyptian queen and a young Hittite prince.

Unfortunately, the foreign prince died before he reached Egypt, so tensions flared up again. There are no signs of trade under the reign of the boy pharaoh. Instead, their armies fought over major cities such as Kadesh, which was the scene of many clashes between the Egyptians and the Hittites and constantly changed hands between the two countries.

Conversely, relations between Egypt and Assyria were good, as the two powers were linked by trade, diplomatic relations and hatred of their shared enemy, the Hittites. Indeed, Assyria also participated in the wars against the Hittites.

Tutankhamun himself deserves some praise for his political decisions. He took small steps towards the renewal of Egypt, and under his reign the country's military efforts began to bear fruit and peace slowly returned to the kingdom. However, it took another 50 years for peace to be fully re-established between the Egyptians and the Hittites thanks to Ramses II (c. 1300-c. 1215 BCE), which in turn restored order and security across the entire kingdom.

KEY MOMENTS

THE RELIGIOUS RESTORATION

Tutankhamun is best-known for restoring the old religion to Egypt, as it was before his father's reign. Once he came to power, Atenism was quickly abandoned. The Restoration Stela, a stone tablet engraved with an edict to this effect, was produced in the first few months of his reign and provides incontestable proof of this religious change.

This law allowed the Egyptian people to return to their old traditions and to the previous polytheistic religion. The former gods were reinstated, the clergy was re-established, the old temples were restored, traditional rites were celebrated once again, and the Egyptian people made more gifts and offerings to the gods. The Stela outlines the steps to be taken to restore the old religion and to make the process easier. The priority was to lift the ban on earlier religious practices so that the Egyptian people could once again enjoy the religious celebrations that were previously the lifeblood of their towns.

Amun was gradually restored to his preeminent place among the Egyptian gods. The capital of Egypt was no longer Akhetaton, as it had been under Akhenaton, but was moved to Thebes. However, given Tutankhamun's extreme youth when he came to power, this decision undoubtedly came from Ay and Horemheb, who were both older and had worshipped the old gods.

NEW CONSTRUCTION PROJECTS

As the region around Thebes was the area that had been most damaged by Akhenaton's labourers, this was where Tutankhamun began his policy of reinstating the old gods by ordering workers to rebuild everything that had been damaged. In Karnak, labourers worked on three major cultural landmarks, namely the Precincts of Amun-Re, Mut and Montu, while in Luxor the main temple was restored.

Tutankhamun also implemented this policy in the Memphis region, near Cairo. The most visible parts of the temples were restored first, while the more hidden parts were left for later restoration campaigns. Throughout the reigns of Tutankhamun and his successor, Ay, labourers worked on these sites to re-engrave the names and images of gods that had been deliberately damaged. Consequently, the extent of the vandalism ordered by Akhenaton in the name of his one god became clear.

A SICKLY ADOLESCENT

Scientists have long believed that Tutankhamun suffered from several physical handicaps. Examination of the many objects discovered in his tomb suggests that he was frail and hunchbacked: over 130 canes, as well as many chairs, stools and armchairs were buried with him. Furthermore, images in the tomb depict the pharaoh sitting in an armchair to shoot a bow and arrow. Given that archery is virtually always practising standing up, it seems that the young pharaoh must have had serious mobility problems.

In 2010, a detailed analysis of Tutankhamun's mummy revealed signs of a club foot, hypophalangism (the absence of one of the bones in the hands or feet) and chronic inflammation due to

Köhler disease (abnormal growth in one of the bones of the feet). As can be imagined, these illnesses did not make it any easier for the young pharaoh to lead his country, as just standing up probably required considerable effort. Travelling by chariot, as was customary for royalty, must also have been difficult and painful. These illnesses probably damaged his hips and pelvis, and may have resulted in scoliosis. This means that Tutankhamun was most likely physically puny, with disproportionately broad hips and a curved back.

AN UNTIMELY DEATH

The young pharaoh died at the age of 20. The cause of his death is difficult to ascertain, as his body bears numerous signs of illnesses and accidents.

In 2005, researchers carried out a CT scan on his body and discovered that his left knee was fractured and had only just begun healing, indicating that the pharaoh died shortly after an accident.

In late 2013, scientists at the Cranfield Institute in England put forward the hypothesis that

Tutankhamun was involved in a chariot crash, as the young pharaoh also had a series of injuries down one side of his body. Some have even suggested that he could have been killed by a charging hippopotamus. However, the causes of his death are ultimately still unclear.

Furthermore, when scientists examined his remains, they discovered the presence of three strains of malaria in the mummy. Given that malaria-carrying mosquitoes are very common in Egypt, it is entirely possible that the sickly young man could have died after being bitten by one.

Whatever the cause, the young pharaoh's sudden death forced his advisors to change their plans for his tomb. The tomb that was initially planned for him was not ready by the time he died, so in the end his successor, Ay, was buried there. Ay was much older than Tutankhamun, and had already begun building his own tomb. Work on this had progressed so much that the decision was taken to bury Tutankhamun in this more modest, but finished, tomb. He still received all the honours that were due to his rank, and his treasures were buried with him in the Valley of the Kings (a region on the banks of the Nile opposite Thebes where the pharaohs of the New Kingdom of Egypt, their wives and children, and some nobles were buried).

THE BURIAL OF A PHARAOH

All sovereigns were buried with items from their everyday lives and objects that had been specially produced to accompany them into the afterlife. Given the magnificent treasure that was buried with the young Tutankhamun, whose reign lasted barely ten years, we can only imagine the treasure that must once have filled the tombs of Amenhotep II (date of birth unknown, date of death c. 1400 BCE) and Ramses II.

Unfortunately, the Valley of the Kings was repeatedly pillaged during antiquity, and Tutankhamun's tomb did not emerge unscathed. It was looted twice, but not long after his death, because the guards of the necropolis subsequently resealed the tomb. The Valley of the Kings was abandoned at the end of the 20th Dynasty, and the mummies and any other valuable objects were transported to two new locations: a tomb known to modern archaeologists as TT320 next to Deir el-Bahri (to the south of the Valley of the Kings, near Thebes), and the tomb of Amenhotep II. This move took place around 1050 BCE under the command of Pinedjem I, the High Priest of Amun at Thebes from 1070 BCE, then pharaoh of Upper Egypt from 1032 BCE.

It had become necessary to transfer the mummies for security reasons, as the pillaging of royal tombs, which had occurred since the earliest days of ancient Egypt, had become difficult to contain by the 11th century BCE. As the tombs in the Valley of the Kings were scattered around a vast mountain, it soon became impossible to keep watch over all of them. The priests of Amun then decided to move the royal mummies and their remaining possessions to a safe place that was known only to the priests.

However, Tutankhamun was not moved at this time, either because he had already been forgotten, or because the treasure buried with him was not considered particularly significant. His tomb ended up buried beneath the rubble and debris from floods and neighbouring construction projects, which actually protected it from looters. It was not until the early 20th century that they young pharaoh was rediscovered and propelled to worldwide fame.

UNSCRUPULOUS LOOTERS

The pillaging of royal tombs has been recorded from the end of the Old Kingdom of Egypt (c. 2700-2200 BCE) onwards. As the power of royalty and the political elite waned, thieves took advantage of this to seize the treasure in the tombs. During the Middle Kingdom of Egypt (2033-1786 BCE), pillaging became a common occurrence, to such an extent that archaeologists have discovered papyrus scrolls bearing accounts of the trials of robbers and the punishments meted out to them: they had their ears or noses cut off, and in some cases they were even sentenced to death.

| Tutankhamun's throne, depicting the young pharaoh in a relaxed pose on his throne, his wife, who is applying ointment to him, and the sun-disc Aten shining down on the royal couple.

A CONTENTIOUS SUCCESSION

After Tutankhamun's death, his former tutor Ay and his general Horemheb fought over the throne. However, Horemheb had to leave in a hurry to repel an attack from their Hittite enemies, leaving Ay free to take the throne while his rival remained a general. It appears that Ay then married the young pharaoh's widow, Ankhesanamun, in order to bolster his legitimacy, since he did not belong to a branch of the royal family that had a rightful claim to the throne. He had been very influential since Akhenaton's reign, and his position as a high-ranking official to the royal family allowed him to become the young Tutankhamun's tutor, but under no circumstances to succeed him.

During his short reign, he pressed on with the return to religious orthodoxy begun by Tutankhamun, which suggests that he may have been behind the restoration of the old faith. Indeed, he was already a powerful figure during the reign of Akhenaton, when Atenism was imposed in Egypt, which means that for much of his life he must have worshipped the old gods. We can surmise that he re-established the religion he had always known as soon as the opportunity arose, as Tutankhamun was much too young to have taken this decision of his own volition.

Ay was already an old man by the time he came to power, and he died around 1320 BCE, allowing Horemheb to finally take the throne. His reign lasted until roughly 1295 BCE, and some of his decisions had a considerable impact in Egypt: he continued and expanded the religious reform begun by Tutankhamun, and restructured part of the country's administration, specifically concerning justice and taxes. These changes provided a foundation for the reigns of his successors.

Horemheb named one of his generals, Paramessu, his heir. Paramessu went on to become Ramses I (died c. 1290 BCE), the first pharaoh of the 19th Dynasty (reigned from 1295 to 1294 BCE) and the grandfather of the great Ramses II. The 18th Dynasty therefore came to an end with the death of Horemheb.

HOREMHEB'S INFLUENCE

Horemheb's political role was so great that the pharaohs of the 19th Dynasty viewed him as a founding father and worshiped him as a semi-divine king, unlike his immediate predecessors.

AN UNPRECEDENTED DISCOVERY

At 10am on 4 November 1922, Howard Carter arrived at the archaeological site in the Valley of the Kings to find the labourers unusually quiet. They had made an exciting discovery: a stone step carved into the rock. The same day, the British archaeologist uncovered the entire step, and then a staircase leading to a door with the seal still intact.

Carter carved a spyhole above the door to try and look in, and saw a corridor filled with material. He immediately realised that he had discovered a place that had remained untouched for millennia.

He immediately informed his friend and patron, Lord Carnarvon (British Egyptologist, 1866-1923), who arrived at the site a few days later with his daughter Evelyn Herbert Beauchamp. The dig resumed, and they uncovered the last two steps and the entirety of the door, which bore the name "Tutankhamun".

However, it soon became clear that the tomb had already been looted, as stones seemed to have been added and the remains of broken seals were found close to the entrance, while another seal was clearly visible on the door. The broken and intact seals were both signed "Maya" (who has been surmised to be the man in charge of the royal necropolis, and the head of the treasury during the reigns of Tutankhamun, Ay and Horemheb). This indicates that the tomb was looted shortly after Tutankhamun's burial.

In spite of the signs of looting, Carter was hopeful that they tomb would be intact, because the great pillages of the Valley of the Kings only began under the reign of Ramses IV (c. 1140-c. 1121 BCE), almost 200 years after Tutankhamun's time. Indeed, Tutankhamun, along with his father and the rest of his family, was never recorded in the royal registers: they were deemed heretics for daring to renounce the old gods, so their names were not recorded for posterity and they soon fell into obscurity. It was therefore highly likely that most of the items buried with Tutankhamun would still be there.

| The Valley of the Kings in 1922.

The researchers cleared the corridor, but their way was barred by a second door, identical to the first. When Carter tried to break through the stone, it immediately gave way and a gust of warm air came through the hole, almost blowing out their candle. Carter managed to reach through the hole with the candle, and even with the flickering light, the gold glinting within was clear to see. Carter was dumbstruck, and remained silent for what must have seemed like an eternity. When he was asked whether there was anything in the tomb, he finally responded

"Yes, wonderful things" (Carter, 2000: 78).

As it turned out, the tomb was packed with thousands of objects: golden statues, grave goods (including beds and a throne), items from everyday life such as jewellery, games, musical instruments and even chariots and weaponry, clothing and textiles, and of course the ancient mummies. For the first time in the history of Egyptology, the treasure within a royal tomb had been discovered almost intact, allowing Egyptologists to gain a better understanding of ancient Egyptian funeral rites.

THE JOURNEY TO THE AFTERLIFE ACCORDING TO EGYPTIAN CUSTOM

The discovery of Tutankhamun's tomb allowed researchers to examine the funerary objects and thus advance their knowledge of funeral rites in ancient Egypt.

Like all pharaohs, the young sovereign's body was treated with the aim of preserving it, so that its Ka (life energy) and Bâ (soul) could rejoin it at the start of its new life. This treatment, known as mummification, was a process comprising several stages lasting a total of 70 days.

To begin with, the body was carefully washed, then most of the internal organs were removed. Next, the priests tasked with the embalming wrapped the body in strips of linen while reciting prayers. In Tutankhamun's case, items of jewellery bearing signs of wear were slipped between these strips, suggesting that they had been worn by the sovereign when he was alive.

During the mummification process, only some of the organs, namely the liver, the stomach, the lungs and the intestines, were kept and placed in canopic jars to protect them for when the pharaoh came back to life.

- The liver was placed under the protection of the human-headed god Imset and the goddess Isis. It was associated with the south.
- The stomach was protected by the jackal-headed god Duamutef and the goddess Neith. It was linked to the east.
- The lungs were under the protection of the baboon-headed god Hapi and the goddess Nephthys. It was associated with the north.
- The intestines were protected by the falcon-

headed god Qebehsenuef and the goddess Sequet. It was related to the west.

The heart was always left in the body.

After these rituals, the body was placed in its sarcophagus and taken to its eternal resting place, where the pharaoh was surrounded by all the objects they needed not only during their life, but also during the afterlife. Indeed, the afterlife was viewed as the continuation of life on earth, which meant that the dead person would carry out the same duties and would need all the objects they normally used or that symbolised their power.

| Howard Carter with Tutankhamun's sarco-
phagus, 1922.

IMPACT

THE GREAT RELIGIOUS RESTORATION

As we have previously explained, the young pharaoh's reign did not stand out for its economic, cultural or political accomplishments, and the greatest achievement of his rule undoubtedly came from Ay and Horemheb, the two key figures in Egypt at this time, rather than Tutankhamun himself. Nonetheless, this religious reformation boosted the country's economy, as artisans worked tirelessly to rebuild temples that had been abandoned or destroyed, and sculptors could now produce statues of all the gods.

THE SCIENTIFIC SIGNIFICANCE OF THE DISCOVERY

The boy pharaoh's impact on future generations was far greater in death than in life. Today, he is known around the world for his opulent treasure, but scientists have also benefitted immensely from the discovery of his tomb.

Researchers have had the opportunity to study objects from ancient Egypt that are almost intact and still in their original context. The vast treasure has allowed them to study gold, metal and silver items, as well as organic materials such as textiles, skin and hair. These decompose much more quickly than metals and are far more vulnerable to variations in temperature, which means that they are much rarer and of greater interest to scientists than gold or silver.

Egypt's arid climate and the protective atmosphere of Tutankhamun's tomb meant that these fragile items were still in excellent condition, which is what makes the discovery so unusual and valuable.

THE CURSE OF THE PHARAOH

The discovery of Tutankhamun's tomb is surrounded by an enduring legend: the curse of the pharaoh, which allegedly struck members of the team who ventured into the royal burial place and doomed them to an untimely death. But was his tomb really protected by a curse?

This legend spread like wildfire, no doubt helped by the particular context of the early 20th century. Spiritism, the belief that it is possible to communicate with the dead, was very popular from the late 19th century onwards, and mummies were part of the collective imagination, meaning that specific powers were commonly ascribed to them at this time. Starting towards the end of the 19th century, a series of mysterious deaths were linked to the Egyptian mummies.

THE MUMMY'S CURSE

The first mummy's curse reportedly struck in 1896. According to a journalist, Walter Herbert Ingram (1855-1888) bought a mummy in Luxor in 1885 and then died in at tragic accident while elephant hunting in Somaliland (former British territory on the Horn of Africa) in 1888. His body was never found. Some claimed that the mummy from Luxor bore a curse promising a violent death with no burial to anyone who desecrated it. The wheels of the curse were then set in motion...

The legend surrounding Tutankhamun's tomb began with the death of Howard Carter's canary, which was swallowed by a cobra. Given that the cobra was the pharaoh's emblem in ancient Egypt, it is not difficult to see why Carter's contemporaries believed that this was an act of vengeance by Tutankhamun.

The legend really blew up in 1923, when Howard Carter's friend and patron Lord Carnarvon died suddenly of pneumonia. The press was quick to add fuel to the fire, whipping readers who had been influenced by Spiritism into a frenzy. Journalists and writers even went so far as to invent an inscription promising death to anyone who entered the pharaoh's tomb. In the years after Tutankhamun's body was removed from the tomb, between 15 and 30 people who were connected to the discovery in some way met with an unexpected end.

| Lord Carnarvon (right) and Howard Carter on the steps leading to Tutankhamun's tomb, 1922.

CURSE OR MYTH?

A closer look at the alleged victims of the curse reveals that there is little connection between the people who died and the discovery itself:

while some had visited the tomb, others had never set foot there. The average age of the "victims" was 52.4, and, given that the average life expectancy in Europe during the 1920s was 52.2., claims of a curse no longer seem credible.

In addition, some of the first researchers on the team lived long lives. Carter himself died of lymphoma at the age of 64, while Lord Carnarvon's daughter, who had been inside the tomb, lived to the age of 79. Many of the Egyptologists who studied the grave goods and inscriptions, and even the scientists who carried out the autopsy on the young pharaoh's mummy, also survived, which further undermines the idea that there was a curse.

AN ENDURING BELIEF

Sir Arthur Conan Doyle (1859-1930), the creator of the famous detective Sherlock Holmes, was a keen Spiritist. He firmly believed that Lord Carnarvon had been killed by an evil spirit, and attested to this conviction in a 1923 New York Times article.

A RATIONAL EXPLANATION

Many scientists have tried to provide rational explanations for these suspicious deaths. An early hypothesis was that the tomb contained germs and bacteria, or even poison that had been placed there by the ancient Egyptian priests.

After several decades of research, in 1999 scientists at the University of Leipzig identified mould spores that could have survived in the darkness for thousands of years and then caused serious illnesses in individuals with weakened immune systems.

In spite of these scientific explanations, the idea of Tutankhamun's curse has never lost its grip on the public imagination. This small story is part of a larger one, and was partly responsible for the spread of the Tutankhamun myth. Even today, articles are written about the legend and are widely read and shared.

"TUTMANIA"

As well as providing a goldmine of unexpected information for Egyptologists, Tutankhamun's treasure also captivated the general public, and countless exhibitions have been dedicated to the young pharaoh.

Tutankhamun Treasures, which was held in the 1960s in cities including Paris and Los Angeles, still ranks as one of the most visited exhibitions of all time. More recently, a major exhibition dedicated to the young pharaoh in Paris in 2012 drew huge visitor numbers. This "Tutmania" can also be seen in the many books, films and video games about the young pharaoh.

Indeed, the years following the discovery of the tomb saw a constant stream of books about pharaohs and curses, including the 1923 short story *The Adventure of the Egyptian Tomb* by the British writer Agatha Christie (1890-1976). The Belgian comic book author Hergé (1907-1983) also drew inspiration from Tutankhamun for two volumes in *The Adventures of Tintin*, *Cigars of the Pharaoh* (1934) and *The Seven Crystal Balls* (1948). More recently, the French novelist and Egyptologist Christian Jacq (born in 1947) has written novels that are largely inspired by the life of Tutankhamun.

The myth of an Egyptian curse appeared in film as early as 1932, with *The Mummy* by Karl Freund (German director, 1890-1969). There are also a number of video games inspired by the legend, including *Uncharted Drake's Fortune* (2007), whose main character falls victim to a curse when he opens a giant golden sarcophagus. These are only a few of the many examples of the influence that Tutankhamun and his curse have exerted over future generations.

SUMMARY

- Tutankhamun was the 11th pharaoh of the 18th Dynasty of Egypt. After his father, Akhenaton, died, he married his sister Ankhesanamun and acceded to the throne.
- He was around seven when he became pharaoh and took power during a period marked by religious change (his father had forced the polytheistic Egyptians to accept a monotheistic religion devoted to the god Aten) and political tensions with the neighbouring Hittites.
- As Tutankhamun was too young to rule, Egypt was controlled by two men: Ay, Tutankhamun's tutor and a high-ranking official in his father's government, and Horemheb, the commander-in-chief of the army. They were the real power behind the throne.
- His reign was cut short by his untimely death at the age of 20, but even so it saw a number of important changes: the former religion, which had been outlawed by his father, was restored, and a period of economic and political renewal began.

- His personal life was also tumultuous, and his life was undoubtedly adversely affected by the various illnesses and physical problems he suffered from. As a child and teenager, his motor abilities must have been impaired, and his illnesses and youth would certainly have stopped him from exercising his power full-time. His fragile constitution was one of the reasons for his early death at around 20 years of age.
- His reign did not leave much of a mark; indeed, no measures were taken to save his tomb from looters, and his contemporaries abandoned it in the Valley of the Kings.
- However, almost 3000 years after his death, the young king has emerged from obscurity to become a global icon. While all Egyptian pharaohs dreamed that they would live on forever and be remembered by future generations, Tutankhamun's name is still with us thousands of years later and he is one of the most famous pharaohs who ever lived.
- The discovery of his tomb is one of the greatest finds in the history of archaeology, both because of the sheer quantity of material and because it had largely escaped the ravages of

time. The impact of this discovery was huge, and is reflected in books, films and popular culture as a whole. More recently, a 2012 exhibition in Paris was a resounding success.

- Popular fascination with the discovery of the tomb is due in large part to the alleged curse that struck the team that found it. However, the sudden, unexpected deaths of some of the researchers could actually be due to mould spores in the tomb, which had been there for thousands of years and proved fatal for individuals with weaker immune systems.

FIND OUT MORE

BIBLIOGRAPHY

- Capart, J. (1923) *Toutânkhamon*. Brussels: Vromant et Cie.

- Carter, H. (2000) *The Discovery of the Tomb of Tutankhamun*. Mineola, New York: Dover Publications, Inc.

- Gabolde, M. (1998) *D'Akhenaton à Toutânkhamon*. Paris: Éditions de Boccard.

- Gabolde, M. (2015) *Toutânkhamon*. Paris: Pygmalion.

- Hawass, Z. (2009) Computed tomographic evaluation of King Tutankhamun, ca. 1300 BC. *Annales du Service des Antiquités de l'Égypte*. 81. Cairo: Imprimerie de l'Institut Français d'Archéologie Orientale, pp. 159-174.

- Nelson, M. (2002) The mummy's curse: historical cohort study. *British Medical Journal*. 325. London: BMJ Publishing, pp. 1482-1484.

- Reeves, N. (1995) *The Complete Tutankhamun: The King · The Tomb · The Royal Treasure*. London: Thames & Hudson.

- Seton, W. (1980) *Le trésor de Toutânkhamon*. Paris:

Édition Princesse.

- Vergote, J. (1961) *Toutânkhamon dans les archives hittites*. Leiden: Istanbul Nederlands Historisch-archaeologisch Instituut in het Nabije Oosten.

ADDITIONAL SOURCES

- Desroches-Noblecourt (1989) *Tutankhamen: Life and Death of a Pharaoh*. London: Penguin.

- Hawass, Z. and Vannini, S. (2007) *King Tutankhamun: The Treasures of the Tomb*. London: Thames & Hudson.

- Harer, B.W. (2006) An explanation of King Tutankhamun's death. *Bulletin of the Egyptian Museum*. 3. Cairo: AUC Press, pp. 83-88.

- James, T.G.C. (2002) *Tutankhamun: The Eternal Splendor of the Boy Pharaoh*. New York: Metro Books.

- Martin, G.T and Strouhal, E. (2008) The Memphite Tomb of Horemheb, Commander-in-chief of Tutankhamun: Human skeletal remains. *Excavation memoir – Egypt Exploration Society*. 55. London: Egypt Exploration Society.

DOCUMENTARIES AND TELEVISION PROGRAMMES

- *Tutankhamun: The Mystery of the Burnt Mummy.* (2013) [Documentary]. Sean Smith. Dir. UK: 3BM Television.

- *Tutankhamun: The Truth Uncovered.* (2014) [Documentary]. Tom Stubberfield. Dir. UK: BBC.

- *Tut.* (2015) [TV miniseries]. David von Ancken. Dir. Canada: Muse Entertainment Enterprises.

LITERATURE

- Christie, A. (2013) *The Adventure of the Egyptian Tomb*. London: HarperCollins.

- Jacq, C. (2003) *The Tutankhamun Affair*. London: Pocket Books.

- Jacq, C. (2009) *Tutankhamun: The Last Secret*. London: Simon & Schuster.

- Rice, A. (1991) *The Mummy Or Ramses the Damned*. New York: Ballantine Books.

ICONOGRAPHIC SOURCES

- Gilded wooden bust of Tutankhamun discovered by Howard Carter in 1922, displayed at the Musem of Cairo. © Jean-Pierre Dalbéra.

- Howard Carter in Chicago, January 1924. Royalty-free reproduction picture.

- Tutankhamun's throne, depicting the young pharaoh in a relaxed pose on his throne, his wife, who is applying ointment to him, and the sun-disc Aten shining down on the royal couple. Royalty-free reproduction picture.

- The Valley of the Kings in 1922. Royalty-free reproduction picture.

- Howard Carter with Tutankhamun's sarcophagus, 1922. Royalty-free reproduction picture.

- Lord Carnarvon (right) and Howard Carter on the steps leading to Tutankhamun's tomb, 1922. Royalty-free reproduction picture.